I0568542

CONCERNING FAITH OF THINGS NOT SEEN

(De fide rerum quæ non videntur)

St. Augustine, Bishop of Hippo

Translated by: C.L. Cornish *(1887)*
Edited by: D.P. Curtin

Dalcassian
Publishing
Company

PHILADELPHIA, PA

All rights reserved. No part of the material protected by this copyright may be reproduced or utilized in any form, electronic or mechanical, including photocopying recording or by any information storage and retrieval system, without written permission from the copyright owner.

Library of Congress Cataloging-in-Publication Data

Copyright © 2018 Dalcassian Publishing Co.
In association with St. Macartan Press
All rights reserved.

This tract was thought spurious by some but is known to be St. Augustine's by his mention of it in Epistle 231 ad Darium Comitem. It seems to have been written after 399, from what is said about Idols, § 10; for in that year Honorius enacted laws against them.

1. There are those who think that the Christian religion is what we should smile at rather than hold fast, for this reason, that, in it, not what may be seen, is shown, but men are commanded faith of things which are not seen. We therefore, that we may refute these, who seem to themselves through prudence to be unwilling to believe what they cannot see, although we are not able to show unto human sight those divine things which we believe, yet do show unto human minds that even those things which are not seen are to be believed. And first they are to be admonished, (whom folly has so made subject to their carnal eyes, as that, whatsoever they see not through them, they think not that they are to believe,) how many things they not only believe but also know, which cannot be seen by such eyes. Which things being without number in our mind itself, (the nature of which mind is incapable of being seen,) not to mention others, the very faith whereby we believe, or the thought whereby we know that we either believe any thing, or believe not, being as it is altogether alien from the sight of those eyes; what so naked, so clear, what so certain is there to the inner eyes of our minds? How then are we not to believe what we see not with the eyes of the body, whereas, either that we believe, or that we believe not, in a case where we cannot apply the eyes of the body, we without any doubt see?

2. But, say they, those things which are in the mind, in that we can by the mind itself discern them, we have no need to know through the eyes of the body; but those things, which you say unto us that we should believe, you

neither point to without, that through the eyes of the body we may know them; nor are they within, in our own mind, that by exercising thought we may see them. And these things they so say, as though any one would be bidden to believe, if that, which is believed, he could already see set before him. Therefore certainly ought we to believe certain temporal things also, which we see not, that we may merit to see eternal things also, which we believe. But, whosoever you are who will not believe save what you see, lo, bodies that are present you see with the eyes of the body, wills and thoughts of your own that are present, because they are in your own mind, you see by the mind itself; tell me, I pray you, your friend's will towards you by what eyes do you see? For no will can be seen by the eyes of the body. What? See you in your own mind this also which is going on in the mind of another? But if you see it not, how do you repay in turn the good will of your friend, if what you cannot see, you believe not? Will you haply say that you see the will of another through his works? Therefore you will see acts, and hear words, but concerning your friend's will, that which cannot be seen and heard you will believe. For that will is not color or figure, so as to be thrown upon the eyes, or sound or strain, so as to glide into the ears; nor indeed is it your own, so as to be perceived by the motion of your own heart. It remains therefore that, being neither seen, nor heard, nor beheld within yourself, it be believed, that your life be not left deserted without any friendship, or affection bestowed upon you be not repaid by you in return. Where then is that which you said, that you ought not to believe, save what you saw either outwardly in the body, or inwardly in the heart? Lo, out of your own heart, you believe an heart not your own; and lendest your faith, where you do not direct the glance of your body or of your mind. Your friend's face you discern by your own body, your own faith you discern by your own mind; but your friend's faith is not loved by you, unless there be in you in return that faith, whereby you may believe that which in him you see not. Although a man may also deceive by feigning good will, and hiding malice: or, if he have no thought to do harm, yet by expecting some benefit from you, feigns, because he has not, love.

3. But you say, that you therefore believe your friend, whose heart you cannot see, because you have proved him in your trials, and have come to know of what manner of spirit he was towards you in your dangers, wherein he deserted you not. Seems it therefore to you that we must wish for our own affliction, that our friend's love towards us may be proved? And shall no man be happy in most sure friends, unless he shall be unhappy through adversity? So that, forsooth, he enjoy not the tried love of the other, unless he be racked by pain and fear of his own? And how in the having of true friends can that happiness be wished for, and not rather feared, which nothing save unhappiness can put to the proof? And yet it is true that a friend may be had also in prosperity, but proved more surely in adversity. But assuredly in order to prove him, neither would you commit yourself to dangers of your own, unless you believed; and thus, when you commit yourself in order to prove, you believe before you prove. For surely, if we ought not to believe things not seen, since indeed we believe the hearts of our friends, and that, not yet surely proved; and, after we shall have proved them good by our own ills, even then we believe rather than see their good will towards us: except that so great is faith, that, not unsuitably, we judge that we see, with certain eyes of it, that which we believe, whereas we ought therefore to believe, because we cannot see.

4. If this faith be taken away from human affairs, who but must observe how great disorder in them, and how fearful confusion must follow? For who will be loved by any with mutual affection, (being that the loving itself is invisible,) if what I see not, I ought not to believe? Therefore will the whole of friendship perish, in that it consists not save of mutual love. For what of it will it be able to receive from any, if nothing of it shall be believed to be shown? Further, friendship perishing, there will be preserved in the mind the bonds neither of marriages, nor of kindreds and relations; because in these also there is assuredly a friendly union of sentiment. Spouse therefore will not be able to love spouse in turn, inasmuch as each believes not the other's love, because the love itself cannot be seen. Nor will they long to have sons, who they believe not will make them a return. And if these be born and grow up, much less will the parents themselves love their own children, whose love towards themselves in those children's hearts they will not see, it being invisible; if it be not praiseworthy faith, but blameable rashness, to believe those things which are not seen. Why should I now speak of the other connections, of brothers, sisters, sons-in-law, and fathers-in-law, and of them who are joined together by any kindred or affinity, if love is uncertain, and the will suspected, that of parents by sons, and that of sons by parents, while due benevolence is not rendered; because neither is it thought to be due, that which is not seen in another not being thought to exist. Further, if this caution be not a mark of ability, but be hateful, wherein we believe not that we are loved, because we see not the love of them who love, and repay not them, unto whom we think not that we owe a return; to that degree are human affairs thrown into disorder, if what we see not we believe not, as to be altogether and utterly overthrown, if we believe no wills of men, which assuredly we cannot see. I omit to mention in how many things they, who find fault with us because we believe what we see not, believe report or history; or concerning places where they have not themselves been; and say not, we believe not, because we have not seen. Since if they say this, they are obliged to confess that their own parents are not surely known to them: because on this point also they have believed the accounts of others telling of it, who yet are unable to show it, because it is a thing already past; retaining themselves no sense of that time, and yet yielding assent without any doubting to others speaking of that time: and unless this be done, there must of necessity be incurred a faithless impiety towards parents, while we are, as it were, showing a rashness of belief in those things which we cannot see. Since therefore, if we believe not those things which we cannot see, human society itself, through concord perishing, will not stand how much more is faith to be applied to divine things, although they be not seen; failing the application of which, it is not the friendship of some men or other, but the very chiefest bond of piety that is violated, so as for the chiefest misery to follow.

5. But you will say, the good will of a friend towards me, although I cannot see it, yet can I trace it out by many proofs; but you, what things you will us to believe not being seen, you have no proofs whereby to show them. In the mean time it is no slight thing, that you confess that by reason of the clearness of certain proofs, some things, even such as are not seen, ought to be believed: for even thus it is agreed, that not all things which are not seen, are not to be believed; and that saying, that we ought not to believe things which we see not, falls to the ground, cast away, and refuted. But they are much deceived, who think that we believe in Christ without any proofs concerning Christ. For what are there clearer proofs than those things, which we now see to have been foretold and fulfilled? Wherefore do ye, who think that there are no proofs why ye ought to believe concerning Christ those things which you have not seen, give heed to what things ye see. The Church herself addresses you out of the mouth of a mother's love: I, whom you view with wonder throughout the whole world, bearing fruit and increasing, was not once such as you now behold me. But, In your Seed shall all nations be blessed. When God blessed Abraham, He gave the promise of me; for throughout all nations in the blessing of Christ am I shed abroad. That Christ is the Seed of Abraham, the order of successive generations bears witness. Shortly to sum up which, Abraham begot Isaac, Isaac begot Jacob, Jacob begot twelve sons, of whom sprung the people Israel. For Jacob himself was called Israel. Among these twelve sons he begot Judah, whence the Jews have their name, of whom was born the Virgin Mary, who bore Christ. And, lo, in

Christ, that is, in the seed of Abraham, that all the nations are blessed, you see and are amazed: and do ye still fear to believe in Him, in Whom ye ought rather to have feared not to believe? What? doubt ye, or refuse ye to believe, the travail of a Virgin, whereas ye ought rather to believe that it was fitting that so God should be born Man. For this also receive ye to have been foretold by the Prophet; Behold, a Virgin shall conceive in the womb, and shall bring forth a Son, and they shall call His Name Emmanuel, which is, being interpreted, God with us. You will not therefore doubt of a Virgin bringing forth, if you be willing to believe of a God being born; leaving not the governance of the world, and coming unto men in the flesh; unto His Mother bringing fruitfulness, not taking away maidenhood. For thus behooved it that He should be born as Man, albeit He was ever God, by which birth He might become a God unto us. Hence again the Prophet says concerning Him, Your Throne, O God, is for ever and ever; a sceptre of right, the sceptre of Your Kingdom. You have loved righteousness, and hated iniquity; therefore God, Your God, has anointed You with the oil of gladness above Your fellows. This anointing is spiritual, wherewith God anointed God, the Father, that is, the Son: whence called from the Chrism, that is, from the anointing, we know Him as Christ. I am the Church, concerning whom it is said to Him in the same Psalm, and what was future foretold as already done; There stood at Your right hand the Queen, in a vesture of gold, in raiment of various colors; that is, in the mystery of wisdom, adorned with various tongues. There it said to me, Hearken, O daughter, and see, and incline your ear, and forget your own people and your father's house: for the King has desired your beauty: seeing that He is the Lord your God: and the daughters of Tyre shall worship Him with gifts, your face shall all the rich of the people entreat. All the glory of that King's daughter is within, in fringes of gold, with raiment of various colors. There shall be brought unto the King the maidens after her; her companions shall be brought unto You. They shall be brought with joy and gladness, they shall be brought into the Temple of the King. Instead of your fathers, there are born unto you sons, you shall set them as princes over the whole earth. They shall be mindful of your name, even from generation to generation. Therefore shall the people confess unto you for ever, and for ever and ever.

6. If this Queen ye see not, now rich also with royal progeny. If she see not that fulfilled which she heard to have been promised, she, unto whom it was said, Hear, O daughter, and see. If she has not left the ancient rites of the world, she, unto whom it was said, Forget your own people and your Father's house. If she confesses not every where Christ the Lord, she, unto whom it was said, The King has desired your beauty, for He is the Lord your God. If she sees not the cities of the nations pour forth prayers and offer gifts unto Christ, concerning Whom it was said to her, There shall worship Him the daughters of Tyre with gifts. If the pride also of the rich is not laid aside, and they do not entreat help of the Church, unto whom it was said, Your face shall all the rich of the people entreat. If He acknowledges not the King's daughter, unto Whom she was bidden to say, Our Father Who art in Heaven; and in her saints in the inner man she is not renewed from day to day, concerning whom it was said, All the glory of that King's daughter is within: although she strike upon the eyes of them also that are without with the blaze

of the fame of her preachers, in diversity of tongues, as in fringes of gold, and raiment of various colors. If there be not, now that His fame is spread abroad in every place by His good odor, virgins also brought unto Christ to be consecrated, of Whom it is said, and to Whom it is said, There shall be brought unto the King the virgins after her, her companions shall be brought unto You. And that they might not seem to be brought like captives, into some, as it were, prison, he says, They shall be brought in joy and gladness, they shall be brought into the King's temple. If she brings not forth sons, that of them she may have, as it were, fathers, whom she may appoint unto herself every where as rulers, she, unto whom it is said, Instead of your fathers there are born unto you sons, you shall set them as princes over the whole earth: unto whose prayers their mother both preferred and made subject, commends herself, They shall be mindful of your name, even from generation to generation. If, by reason of the preaching of those same fathers, wherein they have without ceasing made mention of her name, there are not so great multitudes in her gathered together, and without end in their own tongues unto her confess the praise of grace, unto whom it is said, Therefore shall the people confess unto you for ever, and for ever and ever. If these things are not so shown to be clear, as that the eyes of enemies find not in what direction to turn aside, where the same clearness strikes them not, so as by it to be obliged to confess what is evident: you perhaps assert with reason, that no proofs are shown to you, by seeing which you may believe those things also which you see not. But if those things, which you see, both have been foretold long before, and are so clearly fulfilled; if the truth itself makes itself clear to you, by effects going before and following after, O remnant of unbelief, that you may believe the things which you see not, blush at these things which you see.

7. Give heed unto me, the Church says unto you; give heed unto me, whom you see, although to see ye be unwilling. For the faithful, who were in those times in the land of Judæa, were present at, and learned as present, Christ's wonderful birth of a virgin, and His passion, resurrection, ascension; all His divine words and deeds. These things you have not seen, and therefore ye refuse to believe. Therefore behold these things, fix your eyes on these things, these things which you see reflect on, which are not told you as things past, nor foretold you as things future, but are shown you as things present. What? Seems it to you a vain or a light thing. and think you it to be none, or a little, divine miracle, that in the name of One Crucified the whole human race runs? You saw not what was foretold and fulfilled concerning the human birth of Christ, Behold, a Virgin shall conceive in the womb, and shall bear a Son; but you see the Word of God which was foretold and fulfilled unto Abraham, In your seed shall all nations be blessed. You saw not what was foretold concerning the wonderful works of Christ, Come ye, and see the works of the Lord, what wonders He has set upon the earth: but you see that which was foretold, The Lord said to Me, My Son are You, I have this day begotten You; demand of Me and I will give You nations as Your inheritance, and as Your possession the bounds of the earth. You saw not that which was foretold and fulfilled concerning the Passion of Christ, They pierced My hands and My feet, they numbered all My bones; but they themselves regarded and beheld Me; they divided among them My garments, and upon My vesture they cast the lot; but you see that which was in the same Psalm foretold, and now is clearly fulfilled; All the ends of the earth shall remember and be turned unto

the Lord, and all the kindreds of the nations shall worship in His sight; for the kingdom is the Lord's, and He shall rule over the nations. You saw not what was foretold and fulfilled concerning the Resurrection of Christ, the Psalm speaking, in His Person, first concerning His betrayer and persecutors: They went forth out of doors, and spoke together: against Me whispered all My enemies, against Me thought they evil for Me; they set in order an unrighteous word against Me. Where, to show that they availed nothing by slaying Him Who was about to rise again, He adds and says; What? Will not He, that sleeps, add this, that He rise again? And a little after, when He had foretold, by means of the same prophecy, concerning His betrayer himself, that which is written in the Gospel also, He that did eat of My bread, enlarged his heel upon Me, that is, trampled Me under foot: He straightway added, But do Thou, O Lord, have mercy upon Me, and raise me up again, and I shall repay them. This was fulfilled, Christ slept and awoke, that is, rose again: Who through the same prophecy in another Psalm says, I slept and took my rest; and I rose again, for the Lord will uphold Me. But this ye saw not, but you see His Church, concerning whom it is written in like manner, and fulfilled. O Lord My God, the nations shall come unto You from the extremity of the earth and shall say, Truly our fathers worshipped lying images, and there is not in them any profit. This certainly, whether you want to or not, you behold; even although ye yet believe, that there either is, or was, in those idols some profit; yet certainly unnumbered peoples of the nations, after having left, or cast away, or broken in pieces such like vanities, you have heard say, Truly our fathers worshipped lying images, and there is not in them any profit; shall a man make gods, and, lo, they are no gods? Nor think that it was foretold that the nations should come unto some one place of God, in that it was said, Unto You shall the nations come from the extremity of the earth. Understand, if you can, that unto the God of the Christians, Who is the Supreme and True God, the peoples of the nations come, not by walking but by believing. For the same thing was by another prophet thus foretold, The Lord, says he, shall prevail against them, and shall utterly destroy all the gods of the nations of the earth: and all the isles of the nations shall worship Him, each man from his place. Whereas the one says, Unto You all nations shall come; this the other says, They shall worship Him, each man from his place. Therefore they shall come unto Him, not departing from their own place, because believing in Him they shall find Him in their hearts. You saw not what was foretold and fulfilled concerning the ascension of Christ; Be exalted above the Heavens, O God; but you see what follows immediately after, And above all the earth Your Glory. Those things concerning Christ already done and past, all of them you have not seen; but these things present in His Church ye deny not that you see. Both things we point out to you as foretold; but the fulfillment of both we are therefore unable to point out for you to see, because we cannot bring back into sight things past.

8. But as the wills of friends, which are not seen, are believed through tokens which are seen; thus the Church, which is now seen, is, of all things which are not seen, but which are shown forth in those writings wherein itself also is foretold, an index of the past, and a herald of the future. Because both things past, which cannot now be seen, and things present which cannot be seen all of them, at the time at which they were foretold, no one of these could then be seen. Therefore, since they have begun to come to pass as they were foretold, from those things which have come to pass unto those which are coming to pass, those things which were foretold concerning Christ and the Church have run on in an ordered series: unto which series these pertain concerning the day of Judgment, concerning the resurrection of the dead, concerning the eternal damnation of the ungodly with the devil, and concerning the eternal recompense of the godly with Christ, things which, foretold in like manner, are yet to come. Why therefore should we not believe the first and the last things which we see not, when we have, as witnesses of both, the things between, which we see, and in the books of the Prophets either hear or read both the first things, and the things between, and the last things, foretold before they came to pass? Unless haply unbelieving men judge those things to have been written by Christians, in order that those things which they already believed might have greater weight of authority, if they should be thought to have been promised before they came.

9. If they suspect this, let them examine carefully the copies of our enemies the Jews. There let them read those things of which we have made mention, foretold concerning Christ in Whom we believe, and the Church whom we discern from the toilsome beginning of faith even unto the eternal blessedness of the kingdom. But, while they read, let them not wonder that they, whose are the books, understand not by reason of the darkness of enmity. For that they would not understand was foretold beforehand by the same Prophets; which it behoved should be fulfilled in like manner as the rest, and that by the secret and just judgment of God due punishment should be rendered to their deserts. He indeed, Whom they crucified, and unto Whom they gave gall and vinegar, although when hanging upon the Tree, by reason of those whom He had been about to lead forth from darkness into light, He said to the Father, Forgive them, for they know not what they do; yet by reason of those whom through more hidden causes He had been about to desert, by the Prophet so long before foretold, They gave Me gall for My meat, and in My thirst they gave Me vinegar to drink; let their table become a snare before them, and a recompense, and a stumbling-block: let their eyes be darkened that they see not, and ever bow down their back. Thus, having with them the clearest testimonies of our cause, they walk round about with eyes darkened, that by their means those testimonies may be proved, wherein they themselves are disapproved. Therefore was it brought to pass, that they

should not be so blotted out, as that this same sect should altogether exist not: but it was scattered abroad upon the earth, in order that, carrying with it the prophecies of the grace conferred upon us, more surely to convince unbelievers, it might everywhere profit us. And this very thing which I assert, receive ye after what manner it was prophesied of: Slay them not, says He, lest at any time they forget Your law, but scatter them abroad in Your might. Therefore, they were not slain, in that they forgot not those things which were read and heard among them. For if they were altogether to forget, albeit they understand not, the Holy Scriptures, they would be slain in the Jewish ritual itself; because, when the Jews should know nothing of the Law and of the Prophets, they would be unable to profit us. Therefore they were not slain, but scattered abroad; in order that, although they should not have in faith, whence they might be saved; yet they should retain in their memory, whence we might be helped; in their books our supporters, in their hearts our enemies, in their copies our witnesses.

10. Although, even if there went before no testimonies concerning Christ and the Church, whom ought it not to move unto belief, that the Divine brightness has on a sudden shone on the human race, when we see, (the false gods now abandoned, and their images everywhere broken in pieces, their temples overthrown or changed into other uses, and so many vain rites plucked out by the roots from the most inveterate usage of men,) the One True God invoked by all? And that this has been brought to pass by One Man, by men mocked, seized, bound, scourged, smitten with the palms of the hand, reviled, crucified, slain: His disciples, (whom He chose common men, and unlearned, and fishermen, and publicans, that by their means His teaching might be set forth,) proclaiming His Resurrection, His Ascension, which they asserted that they had seen, and being filled with the Holy Ghost, sounded forth this Gospel, in all tongues which they had not learned. And of them who heard them, part believed, part, believing not, fiercely withstood them who preached. Thus while they were faithful even unto death for the truth, strove not by returning evil, but by enduring, overcame not by killing, but by dying; thus was the world changed unto this religion, thus unto this Gospel were the hearts of mortals turned, of men and women, of small and great, of learned and unlearned, of wise and foolish, of mighty and weak, of noble and ignoble, of high and low, and, throughout all nations the Church shed abroad so increased, that even against the Catholic faith itself there arises not any perverse sect, any kind of error, which is found so to oppose itself to Christian truth, as that it affect not and go not about to glory in the name of Christ: which very error would not be suffered to spring up throughout the earth, were it not that the very gainsaying exercised an wholesome discipline. How would The Crucified have availed so greatly, had He not been God that took upon Him Man, even if He had through the Prophet foretold no such things to come? But when now this so great mystery of godliness has had its prophets and heralds going before, by whose divine voices it was before proclaimed; and when it has come in such manner as it was before proclaimed, who is there so mad as to assert that the Apostles lied concerning Christ, of Whom they preached that He had come in such manner as the Prophets foretold afore that He should come, which Prophets were not silent as to true things to come concerning the Apostles themselves? For concerning these they had said, There is neither speech nor language, whereof their voices are not heard; their sound went out into all the earth, and their words unto the ends of the world. And this at any rate we see fulfilled in the world, although we have not yet seen Christ in the flesh. Who therefore, unless blinded by amazing madness, or hard and steeled by amazing obstinacy, would be unwilling to put faith in the sacred Scriptures, which have foretold the faith of the whole world?\

11. But you, beloved, who possess this faith, or who have begun now newly to have it, let it be nourished and increase in you. For as things temporal have come, so long before foretold, so will things eternal also come, which are promised. Nor let them deceive you, either the vain heathen, or the false Jews, or the deceitful heretics, or also within the Catholic (Church) itself evil Christians, enemies by so much the more hurtful, as they are the more within us. For, lest on this subject also the weak should be troubled, divine prophecy has not been silent, where in the Song of Songs the Bridegroom speaking unto the Bride, that is, Christ the Lord unto the Church, says, As a lily in the midst of thorns, so is my best Beloved in the midst of the daughters. He said not, in the midst of them that are without; but, in the midst of daughters. Whoever has ears to hear, let him hear: and while the net which is cast into the sea, and gathers together all kinds of fishes, as says the holy Gospel, is being drawn unto the shore, that is, unto the end of the world, let him separate himself from the evil fishes, in heart, not in body; by changing evil habits, not by breaking sacred nets; lest they who now seem being approved to be mingled with the reprobate, find, not life, but punishment everlasting, when they shall begin on the shore to be separated.

www.ingramcontent.com/pod-product-compliance
Lightning Source LLC
Chambersburg PA
CBHW070958120626
46546CB00004B/1686